COMET CATCHER

JOHN PERRITANO

red rhino
b**OO**ks®
NONFICTION

3D Printing

Area 51

Bioweapons

Cannibal Animals

Cloning

Comet Catcher

Drones

Fault Lines

Gnarly Sports Injuries

Great Spies of the World

Hacked

Little Rock Nine

Medal of Honor

Monsters of the Deep

Monsters on Land

The Science of Movies

Seven Wonders of the
  Ancient World

Tuskegee Airmen

Virtual Reality

Wild Weather

Witchcraft

Wormholes

All source images from Shutterstock.com

SADDLEBACK
EDUCATIONAL PUBLISHING
www.sdlback.com

ISBN-13: 978-1-68021-047-7
ISBN-10: 1-68021-047-5
eBook: 978-1-63078-374-7

Printed in Malaysia

22 21 20 19 18   1 2 3 4 5

TABLE OF CONTENTS

"3, 2, 1."

Blast off!

Engines roar.

The ground shakes.

Fire burns.

Smoke builds.

A rocket takes off.

It flies high.

People watch.

The rocket gets smaller.

It is going to space.

Something is inside.

It is a *spacecraft*.

A big job waits.

The craft will go far.

It will take ten years.

Then it will catch a *comet*.

3

Chapter 2
WHAT ARE COMETS?

Our *solar system* is old.
Scientists have an idea.
This is called a *theory*.

It was long ago.
There was a cloud.
It was huge.
The cloud spun around.
Rocks were inside.
Dust, gas, and ice were too.

Our sun was made.
Planets were next.
Then came comets.
They came from what was left.

THE SCIENCE OF COMETS

Scientists believe that our solar system was created 4.6 billion years ago.

Famous Comets

Comet McNaught

It was discovered in 2006. This is one of the brightest comets that has been found. In some places, people could see it without a telescope during the day. Comet McNaught takes 92,600 years to orbit the sun.

Chapter 3
SECRETS OF COMETS

Comets are special.
Many think so.
They hold clues.
We can learn things.
How did life begin?

Some have an idea.
Comets flew in space.
They carried *carbon*.

Carbon is in all living things.
It is needed for life.
People have it.
Animals do too.
Even plants have it.

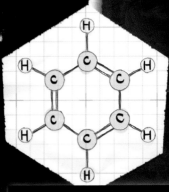
Carbon molecule structure

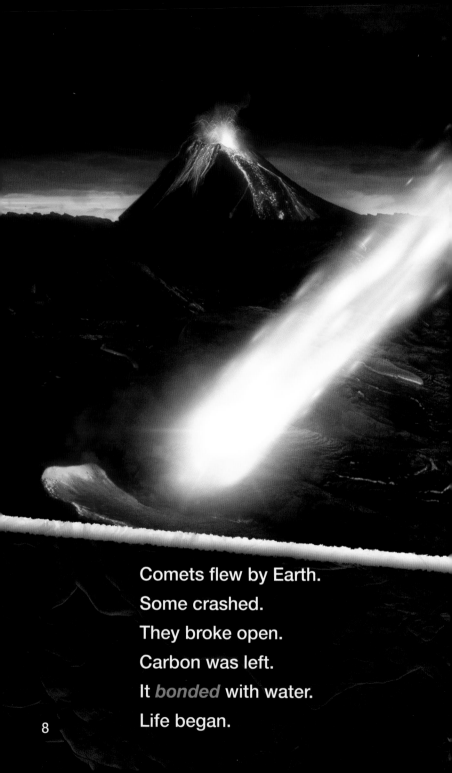

Comets flew by Earth.
Some crashed.
They broke open.
Carbon was left.
It *bonded* with water.
Life began.

Famous Comets

Hale-Bopp

It was discovered in 1995. Scientists spotted it just outside Jupiter's orbit. The brightness made it easy for people to see without a telescope. Hale-Bopp was visible for a record 18 months.

But we need proof.

Comets might have it.

This is one reason to study them.

Chapter 4
ATCHING A COMET

We look to the skies.

Comets are tiny.

They look like a speck.

We use a tool.

t is called a *telescope*.

This helps us see them.

Many want to know more.

nformation is needed.

t must come from a comet.

How can they get it?

People can't go.

They would die.

But a craft could go.

t could send back facts.

Comets are fast.

They move 300 miles a second.

One could go from Boston to New York City.

It would take a second.

Catching one would be hard.

Scientists worked on this.

They had an idea.

A craft could get to a comet.

It would need a *lander*.

Anchors could hold it.

Then it could get facts.

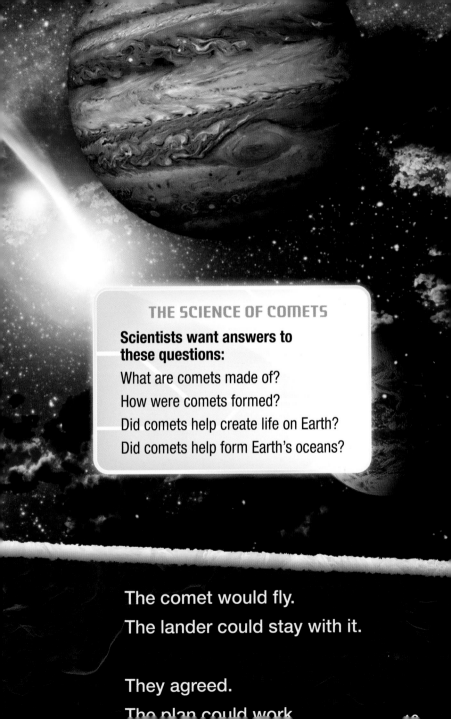

THE SCIENCE OF COMETS

Scientists want answers to these questions:

What are comets made of?

How were comets formed?

Did comets help create life on Earth?

Did comets help form Earth's oceans?

The comet would fly.

The lander could stay with it.

They agreed.

The plan could work.

Chapter 5

THE PLAN

It was the 1980s.

A team was made.

It was in Europe.

Scientists were on the team.

There were engineers too.

They planned.

A craft would fly to space.

It would catch a comet.

Two crafts were needed.

One was called *Rosetta*.

Famous Comets

Halley's Comet

It was discovered in 1758 and named after Sir Edmond Halley. This comet orbits the sun every 76 years. It was bright in 1910. But it was a dud in 1986.

Rosetta was a special name.
It came from a rock.
The rock was a big deal.

It was 1799.
French soldiers were in Egypt.
They found a stone.
There were marks on it.
People studied them.
They learned about the past.
The rock was given a name.
It was called the Rosetta Stone.

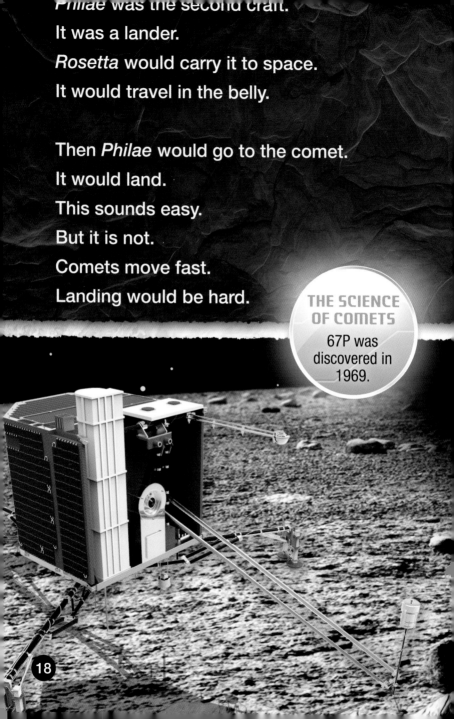

Philae was the second craft.
It was a lander.
Rosetta would carry it to space.
It would travel in the belly.

Then *Philae* would go to the comet.
It would land.
This sounds easy.
But it is not.
Comets move fast.
Landing would be hard.

THE SCIENCE
OF COMETS

67P was
discovered in
1969.

But there was more.

How would it stay on?

It needed hooks.

They would hold it in place.

Then the real work would start.

Philae would collect information.

The team would learn.

The team chose a comet.

It was 67P.

Chapter 6
THE COMET

Many think comets are round.

But they are not.

They crash into other comets.

Bits break off.

Most have odd shapes.

67P looks like a duck.

THE SCIENCE OF COMETS

Some call comets dirty snowballs.

Quack! Quack!

67P is like most comets.

The *core* is ice.

Rocks, gas, and dust are on top.

It is 2.5 miles by 2.7 miles.

Craters cover it.

There are steep cliffs.

It has huge boulders too.

PARTS OF A COMET

tail: made from dust particles; sometimes people can see a comet's tail from Earth

core: center of the comet; this is mostly ice

coma: the comet's atmosphere that covers the core; this is made of rocks, gas, and dust

67P travels around the sun.
Each trip is called an *orbit*.
An orbit takes more than six years.

The team had a question.
When would 67P be near the sun?
That was the best time to reach it.
They did research.
The answer was 2014.

The trip would be long.
It would take ten years.
They should *launch* in 2004.

Time to orbit the sun

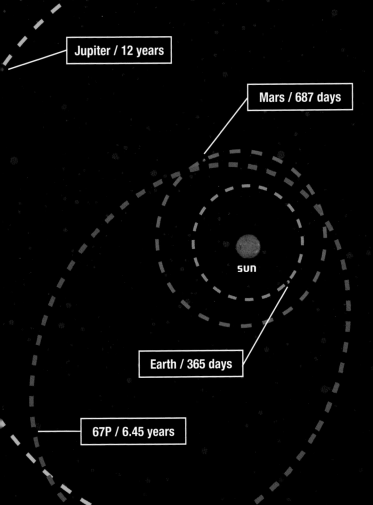

Jupiter / 12 years

Mars / 687 days

SUN

Earth / 365 days

67P / 6.45 years

23

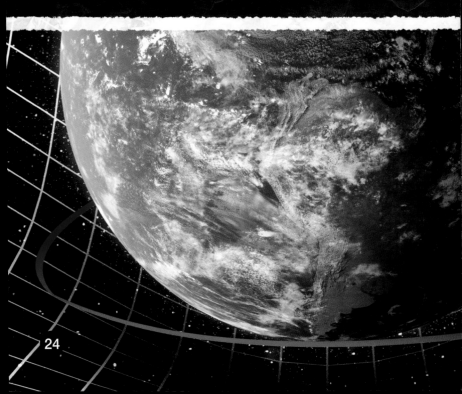

Chapter 7

THE LONG TREK

No rocket could catch 67P.

The comet was too fast.

But the team found a way.

Rosetta launched.

It flew through the solar system.

Some say it was like a game of pool.

It knocked around like a pool ball.

Rosetta circled the sun four times.

It flew near Earth three times.

Then it flew by Mars once.

This was on purpose.

It helped with speed.

How?

Planets have *gravity*.

So does the sun.

They pulled *Rosetta* close.

The craft moved faster.

Then it zoomed away.

This was like a slingshot.

Danger was ahead.

There is an *asteroid* belt.

It is between Mars and Jupiter.

Many call it the Main Belt.

The Main Belt was risky.

There are billions of asteroids.

Some are tiny.

They are like pebbles.

Others are huge.

They could have hit the craft.

It would have been wrecked.

The mission would be over.

Rosetta passed through it.

No other craft had done that.

Rosetta was the first.

Famous Comets

Great Daylight Comet of 1910

It was discovered in January 1910. Workers at a South African diamond mine first spotted it. It was visible for months.

The team chose a spot.
Rosetta and 67P would meet.
But they wouldn't arrive at the same time.

Rosetta flew.
It took seven years.
Finally it got there.
But the comet was not close.
Rosetta had to wait for it.

There was a reason.
This saved power.
Solar panels helped.
They got energy from the sun.
It was turned into electricity.

The team talked to *Rosetta*.
This happened all the time.
They sent *signals*.
Rosetta sent signals back.
They were updates.
Here's where we are.
This is what we're doing.
We learned something.
The process was slow.
Signals had to go a long way.
Sometimes it took an hour.

Rosetta waited.

67P got closer.

It was still far away.

But it was close enough to study.

The team used a special tool.

It was called Alice.

Alice aimed its beam at the comet.

The beam split its light.

The team looked at the colors.

They learned about the *coma*.

This is the comet's atmosphere.

Now they knew what it was made of.

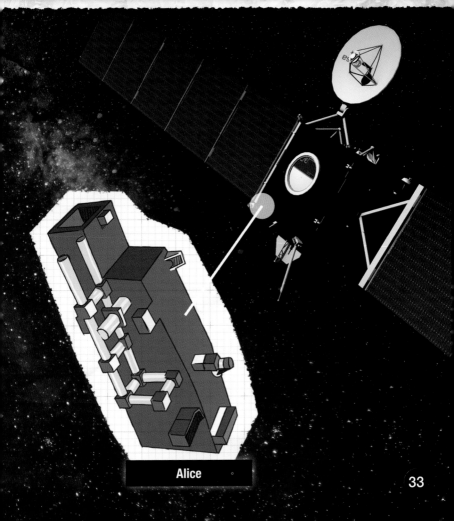

Alice

The team had another job.
Philae would need a safe place to land.
Rosetta aimed its camera.
It took pictures of the comet.
The team studied them.
They found a good spot.
It was smooth.
There were few rocks.
It was not too hot.
There was good sunlight.
That was a big deal.
The sun was needed for power.

The comet kept moving.
Rosetta slept.
It saved power.
That power would be needed soon.

It was January 2014.
Rosetta woke up.
Its rockets fired.
This slowed the craft.
It *drifted*.

36

Months went by.

It was November 12, 2014.

There was 67P.

It had finally arrived.

Rosetta had traveled a long way.

The trip was 3.7 billion miles.

The belly of the craft opened.

There was *Philae*.

It was time for the next phase.

The team watched.

They were on high alert.

Philae had to get to the comet.

67P moved fast.

The landing could be rough.

Would *Philae* make it?

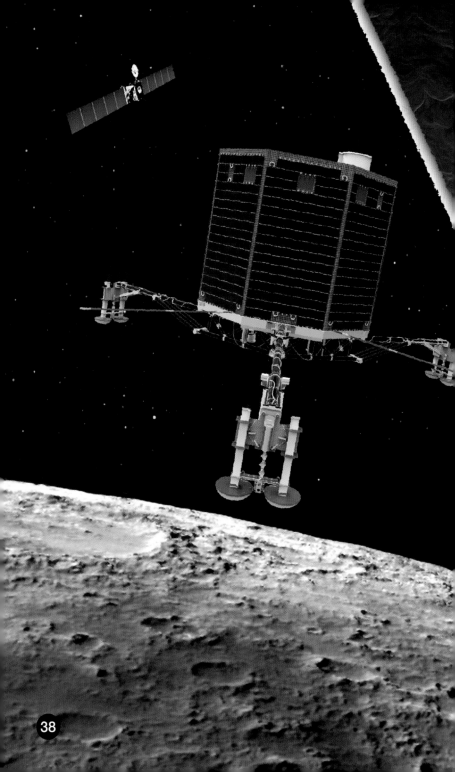

Chapter 8
CONTACT

It was time.

The team launched the lander.

Philae flew to 67P.

The comet's gravity pulled it close.

The lander had to hook onto the comet.

It tried to shoot out anchors.

Nothing happened.

It tried again.

This time they worked.

Anchors shot out.

They grabbed hold of 67P.

The anchors pulled the craft down.

Philae bounced.
It bumped once.
Then it bumped again.
Finally it stopped.
Philae had landed.

But there was a problem.
Philae was in the wrong place.
It had missed its mark.
Philae was in the shade.
That was bad.
The lander needed sunlight.
It kept the power going.

The sun did not reach *Philae*.
Its batteries shut down.
They could not recharge.
Philae went to sleep.
It slept for seven months.

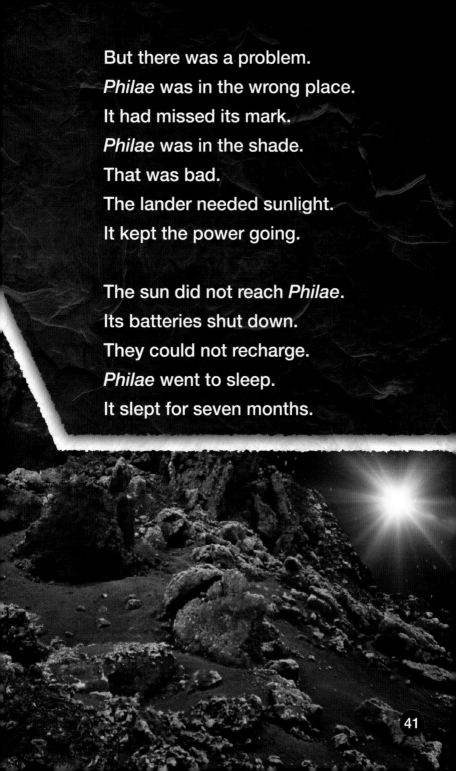

Chapter 9
EXPLORING

It was June 14, 2015.

Philae woke up.

The comet had turned.

Now the sun was closer.

Sunlight shined on *Philae*.

It hit the solar panels.

The batteries turned on.

Philae started working.

The team was happy.

Rosetta had caught the comet.

Philae had landed.

Now it had power.

It could do its job.

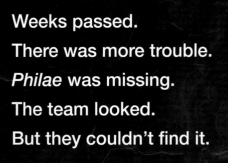

Weeks passed.
There was more trouble.
Philae was missing.
The team looked.
But they couldn't find it.

It was September 2, 2015.
The team found *Philae*.
The craft was stuck.
It was in a deep crack.

Rosetta's crash

It was September 30, 2015.

The team decided.

It was time to crash _Rosetta_.

The craft flew into 67P.

It blew up.

The mission was over.

Famous Comets

Comet Kohoutek

It was discovered in 1973. Scientists thought it was going to be very bright. They called it the "Comet of the Century." But it didn't live up to its nickname.

Philae wasn't on the comet long.

But it did good work.

The team learned.

The comet's core is ice.

Dust covers the ice.

Some gases were found.

Organic matter was too.

But there are still questions.

There is much to learn.

Will there be more missions?

Many hope so.

There are plans.

One goal is to catch another comet.

But there is a bigger goal.

They want to study a comet up close.

This would be hard.

A chunk would have to be collected.

Then it would be brought back.

Can we do this?

Time will tell.

One thing we know for sure.

Comets have much to teach us.

GLOSSARY

anchor: a heavy device that is used to hold something in place

asteroid: a small object that orbits the sun

bond: a force that connects two elements together

carbon: an element that is in all living things

coma: the atmosphere of a comet; it surrounds the core

comet: an object in space that is made of dust, gas, rocks, and ice

core: the center of an object

crater: a large hole in the ground

drift: to move slowly from one place to another

gravity: the force of attraction between two objects in space

lander: a spacecraft designed to land on an object in space

launch: to send something into outer space

orbit: the curved path that something follows as it circles another object in space

organic: something that comes from or is related to living things

signal: a message, sound, or image that travels through space

solar panel: a piece of equipment that uses energy from the sun to create electricity

solar system: our sun and planets that orbit around it; includes other smaller bodies in space like comets and asteroids

spacecraft: a vehicle that is used to travel in outer space

telescope: a device that makes distant objects such as stars appear closer

theory: an idea that explains facts or events

TAKE A LOOK INSIDE

3D PRINTING

A 3D World: In 2016, an 11-year-old from Michigan printed a working violin in his own home. He now plans to start his own 3D-printed violin business.

Material for 3D printing

3D printers are different.
They print a *layer*.
Another layer is added.
This keeps going.
It can happen millions of times.

The layers build.
An object takes shape.
Finally it is ready to use.

3D printers make tools.
One studies breath.
It tests for *diseases*.
Cancers can be found.
Other diseases can too.
The tool is cheap.
Other tests cost more.
This saves money.

Body parts can be printed.
Ears are easy.
Noses are too.
They are mostly soft tissue.
It is called *cartilage*.
Other body parts are harder to print.
Not all can be made yet.

A 3D World Researchers in Spain have developed a printer that will print human skin.

3D printer

Chapter 10
WHAT'S NEXT?

3D printing brings changes.
Food is changing.
People are printing food.
It may be eaten in space.
It could feed soldiers too.
Could this help the hungry?

3D printers solve crimes.
They cause some too.
Will laws be passed to help with this?

The way things are made is changing.
Some have been hard to make.
3D printers make it easy.
Models are cheaper.
Companies can try more ideas.

red rhino books®

NONFICTION

9781680210736

9781680210316

9781680210729

9781680210484

9781680210347

9781680210477

9781680210293

9781680210538

9781680210712

9781680210491

9781680210378

9781680210552